Trumpet
Globetrotters
12 pieces in styles from around the world

Shanti Paul Jayasinha

MUSIC DEPARTMENT

OXFORD
UNIVERSITY PRESS

10.9

OXFORD
UNIVERSITY PRESS

Great Clarendon Street, Oxford OX2 6DP, England

Oxford University Press is a department of the University of Oxford.
It furthers the University's aim of excellence in research, scholarship,
and education by publishing worldwide

This collection © Oxford University Press 2013

Shanti Paul Jayasinha has asserted his right under the Copyright, Designs
and Patents Act, 1988, to be identified as Author of this Work

Database right Oxford University Press (maker)

First published 2013

1 3 5 7 9 10 8 6 4 2

ISBN 978-0-19-338622-8

Music and text origination by Julia Bovee
Printed in Great Britain on acid-free paper by
Halstan & Co. Ltd., Amersham, Bucks.

All the tunes in this book are original pieces by Shanti Paul Jayasinha.

Author acknowledgements: Shanti would like to thank Philip Croydon and Laura Jones for guiding
him through the process, Philip Croydon and Nikki Iles for their contributions to the piano scores,
Clare Foster and Maia Jayasinha for their listening skills, his students for being willing guinea pigs,
and all the musicians who played on the CD.

CD credits: Shanti Paul Jayasinha (trumpet, Flügelhorn, maracas, güiro, keyboards, penny whistle,
recording and mixing engineer), Paul Taylor (trombone), Oren Marshall (tuba), Stewart Curtis (piccolo,
clarinet, alto sax, tenor sax), Clare Foster (clarinet), Mick Foster (alto sax, baritone sax, clarinet),
Ros Stephen (violin), Martina Schwarz (accordion), John Crawford (piano, electric piano),
Guillermo Hill (guitars), Simon Edwards (bass guitar, acoustic bass guitar, Cuban baby bass),
Kuljit Bhamra (dhad, dholak, shakers, tabla), Davide Giovannini (drums), Paul Rumbol (cavaquinho),
Güneş Cerit (saz), Yulexmis Ricaño (tres), Ronen Kozocaro (Egyptian daf, frame drum, tambourine).

Contents

Take a thrilling journey around the world with this collection of 12 fun, original pieces. Suitable for trumpet players of 2+ years' experience (around grade 2 to 5 standard), the pieces are based on a wide variety of world-music styles.

Each piece comes with background information about the musical style and warm-up exercises to help with the specific demands of the music.

The accompanying CD includes authentic performance and play-along tracks for each piece, recorded by a band of world-music specialists.

Trumpet accompaniment parts, suitable for a more advanced player or teacher, are provided for every piece, and piano accompaniments (with guitar chord symbols) for printing are included on the CD as PDFs. PC users can access the PDFs by selecting 'Computer' from the start-up menu and right-clicking on the CD drive to open the CD. Mac users should double-click on the data disc that appears when the CD is inserted to see the PDF files.

1. Princess Therese

Globetrotters
GERMANY

Like a waltz ♩ = 160

German 'oompah' music comes from Bavaria and is played by wind bands that include clarinet, trumpet, trombone, tuba, and accordion. The tuba plays on the beat—the 'oom'—and the clarinet, accordion, or trombone play the 'pah'. If the music has three beats in a bar, as this piece does, it becomes 'oompah-pah'. Oompah bands play several types of dance music, among them polkas, schottisches, waltzes, and ländlers. Every September–October there is a huge beer festival in Munich (the Oktoberfest), with lots of oompah bands. These festivals date back to the wedding in 1810 of Therese von Sachsen-Hildburghausen and Crown Prince Ludwig of Bavaria.

Trumpet accompaniment

5

2. Song for Sabahat

* Use the third valve with the tuning slide pushed out 1.5–2 cm to play the E half-flats.

A piano accompaniment for printing is included on the CD (see page 3).

Turkish folk music often uses the quarter-tone, an interval half the size of a semitone. It is also often in unusual time signatures, with five, seven, or nine beats in a bar. Try Warm-ups 2a and 2b, p. 28, to practise tuning the E half-flats and to get a feel for the melody (the beats in each bar are divided 3 + 2 + 2). Traditional instruments include the *saz* (a kind of lute), *duduk* (double reed), *sipsi* (single reed, like a clarinet), *kaval* and *ney* (end-blown flutes), *darbuka* and *daf* (drums), and violin. The inspiration for this tune came from Sabahat Akkiraz, a well-known Turkish female singer. Turkish melodies are meant to be performed with a lot of expression and emotion, so try to play this piece very soulfully.

Trumpet accompaniment

Globetrotters
SOUTH AFRICA

3. Mongezi

Shuffle ♩ = 126 (♫ = ♪³♪)

A piano accompaniment for printing is included on the CD (see page 3).

During the 1920s–60s in the urban townships of South Africa, musicians fused African melody with jazz improvisation to create 'township jazz'. Music was very important to the people and accompanied all aspects of life, from herding cattle to simply walking home. Some of the leading musicians and composers of this style of jazz are Abdullah Ibrahim, Chris McGregor, and the trumpeter Mongezi Feza, after whom this piece is named. Their bands featured piano, bass, drums, percussion, saxophones, trumpets, and whistles. This piece has a very groovy swing rhythm and should be played with panache! Use the warm-ups on p. 29 to practise your swing rhythms.

Trumpet accompaniment

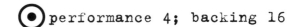

Rhythmic waltz feel ♩ = 144

A piano accompaniment for printing is included on the CD (see page 3).

© Oxford University Press 2013. Photocopying this copyright material is ILLEGAL.

10

Mariachi is a form of folk music from Mexico played by an ensemble of string instruments and trumpets. The string instruments are usually violins and guitars, perhaps including a guitarrón mexicano (bass guitar) and a Mexican vihuela (a high-pitched guitar with a round back). Trumpets are a more modern addition to the line-up, but now play a prominent role in the music. Members of mariachi groups wear distinctive embroidered uniforms derived from the costumes worn by Mexican horse riders known as charros. '¡Bien hecho!' (which means 'well done!') is in the style of a canción ranchera, or 'ranch song', and has a strong waltz-like feel. The staccato notes should be as short as possible (see Warm-up 4, p. 29).

Trumpet accompaniment

Mournfully ♩. = 54

A piano accompaniment for printing is included on the CD (see page 3).

New Orleans has a rich musical heritage, based mainly on African singing styles and European hymn tunes. At the start of the twentieth century many benevolent societies were formed. People would pay in a small amount each week, and in turn their funerals were taken care of, and they were helped when they were sick. These societies would march and play during funeral processions and at Mardi Gras celebrations. This tune is a dirge, which is a beautiful, slow, sad song at the start of a funeral procession. It requires excellent breath control and a well-controlled vibrato (See Warm-ups 5b and 5c, p. 29).

Trumpet accompaniment

performance 6; backing 18

Paso doble is a Spanish dance and music form typically played at bull-fights and town fiestas (parties). It is a bold and decisive style that originated in the military marches of the nineteenth century. The paso doble dance is performed by couples, where the man plays the bull fighter and the woman plays his cape. Spanish town bands are usually wind bands with flutes, clarinets, saxophones, brass, and percussion. This piece—named after the bustling square in central Madrid—is fast and exciting and requires clean, crisp tonguing (see Warm-up 6, p. 30).

Trumpet accompaniment

15

7. East Broadway and Jefferson

Globetrotters
KLEZMER, E. EUROPE

Lively ♩ = 126

A

* last time (opt.):　　　　　　　　　　† last time (opt.):

A piano accompaniment for printing is included on the CD (see page 3).

Klezmer is Jewish music from eastern Europe and is characterized by expressive melodies, usually in minor keys, set against a strongly rhythmic accompaniment. When Jewish immigrants went to New York in the early twentieth century they continued playing and writing klezmer music. This piece is a freylekhs (pronounced 'fray-lacks', a Yiddish word meaning 'joyful'), which is a fast dance piece. It should be played very energetically. Klezmer music is full of grace notes, bends, and slurs. In this piece suggested grace notes are written in, but you can add more or leave some out if you prefer. Warm-up 7, p. 30, explains how to play the ornaments.

Trumpet accompaniment

17

8. Jugando con el son

Globetrotters

CUBA

* Improvise using these pitches (in any order) as a guide.

A piano accompaniment for printing is included on the CD (see page 3).

The Cuban 'son' brings together elements of African and Spanish music to form a style that is often called Afro-Cuban. A typical son group, or *conjunto*, consists of guitar, tres (Cuban guitar), bongos, claves, maracas, voices, trumpet, congas, and piano. The African influence can be seen in the son rhythms, based around the five-note clave pattern (see Warm-up 8, p. 30), and in the call-and-response structure; the guitars and harmony reflect the Spanish influence. The melody in 'Jugando con el son' (or 'Playing with son') comes from both roots. If you feel confident, try improvising a solo at letter D; the CD provides an example.

Trumpet accompaniment

* The small notes should be played second time only.

A piano accompaniment for printing is included on the CD (see page 3).

This piece is based on an Indian scale (raga) called Gaud Malhar. Melody is very important in Indian music, and the different ragas each create a different mood in the listener. According to the legend, Malhar is so powerful that when sung, rain falls from the sky. You can see the Gaud Malhar raga, and some characteristic phrases from it, in the warm-ups on p. 31. The groove of this piece is Bhangra, which is slightly swung. It is normally played on a *dhol*, a popular folk drum of northern India, Pakistan, and Bangladesh. It is a barrel-shaped, sometimes cylindrical drum, with skins on both sides. One side of the drum has a high pitch and the other side has a lower pitch.

Trumpet accompaniment

21

10. Anikulapo, Kini Tuntun

Globetrotters
WEST AFRICA

Lively and rhythmic ♩ = 84

A piano accompaniment for printing is included on the CD (see page 3).

Afrobeat is a style of African popular music, fusing the traditional music of the Yoruba people of West Africa with modern styles including jazz and funk. The music is very rhythmic (see Warm-up 10), with an emphasis on repetition, and the chanted lyrics often have a political message. The term 'Afrobeat' was coined by Nigerian musician Fela Kuti, who developed the style in the 1960s. The title of this piece ('Anikulapo, what's new?') is a reference to Kuti's middle name: Anikulapo. Afrobeat bands tend to be quite large, with guitars, bass, drums, percussion, keyboards, horns, and vocals. Drums, bass, guitar, and percussion create a continuous groove, with other parts layering up to create a long crescendo.

Trumpet accompaniment

Globetrotters SERBIA

11. August in Guča

Fast and exuberant ♩ = 152

*This ornament is notated as semiquavers throughout, but should be played as ♫ ; see Warm-up 11a.

Village brass bands are popular in Serbia and across the Balkans, where they play at weddings and other important events. Fast and exuberant, the music is performed on a large collection of brass instruments, including trumpets and Flügelhorns, accompanied by drums. Serbian brass players use a lot of ornaments. Try Warm-up 11a, p. 32, to practise the 'long-short, long-short' ornament—notated here as a group of four semiquavers. The annual Guča (pronounced 'Gootcha') trumpet festival takes place every August, with all the best Serbian bands competing.

Trumpet accompaniment

* This ornament is notated as semiquavers throughout, but should be played as ♪; see Warm-up 11a.

A piano accompaniment for printing is included on the CD (see page 3).

* An alternative, advanced version of this piece with duet or piano accompaniment is available for printing from the CD, with performance and backing (CD tracks 25 and 26) also included.

A piano accompaniment for printing is included on the CD (see page 3).

In Rio de Janeiro, Brazil, there is a great tradition of brass players playing choros ('cry' or 'lament') and chorinhos ('little cry' or 'little lament'). Choros and chorinhos are considered to be the earliest form of Brazilian popular music and display the influences of African and European classical music. The rhythm is like a samba, and the melodies are very sophisticated, with lots of counterpoint from the backing instruments. The title of this piece ('Sinuous') describes the many twists and turns the music takes as it changes key from section to section. If you feel confident, try the advanced version of this piece included on the CD (see page 3).

Trumpet accompaniment

1. Princess Therese

STACCATO AND LEGATO

In this piece see if you can make a real difference between the staccato, tongued 'oompah' sections and the smooth legato sections. Practise this with the following exercises:

Ex.i

Ex.ii

For the legato sections, you'll need to take big, deep breaths. Try breathing out before you take the first breath in, and then let your lungs fill up naturally. When you feel comfortable playing four bars in one breath, see if you can manage eight bars.

2. Song for Sabahat

(a) QUARTER-TONES

This piece uses a Turkish scale, or 'makam', which includes quarter-tones—notes you don't find on a piano! Practise this exercise to help you tune the E half-flats in the melody. Count in four steady beats, then listen to the note played on CD track 27 before playing it yourself. Push your third-valve tuning slide out 2 cm until the E half-flat is in tune. Notice how the note becomes slightly lower as the slide moves further out.

listen   play etc.

(b) 7/4 EXERCISE

Turkish music often has five, six, seven, or nine beats in a bar. Sing the opening melody using the words below; the bar is divided 3 + 2 + 2.

I want to play with my friends and go to the field to run then we'll kick a foot - ball.

3. Mongezi

RHYTHM EXERCISES

This piece has a swing or shuffle feel, where the quavers are played with the 'long-short' rhythm shown below:

Written:

Played:

Practise playing swing rhythms in the following exercises, which will also help you to improve your syncopation.

Ex. i   *Ex. ii*

Ex. iii

4. ¡Bien hecho!

STACCATO PRACTICE

This exercise will help with your staccato playing. Work up the scale as shown until you get to a starting note of B, then come back down in the same way. Try to make the notes as short as possible by dropping and immediately lifting the tongue, as if saying 'tut'.

5. Marching Down St Claude

(a) TWO- AND THREE-BEAT PATTERNS

With your metronome set to ♩. = 54, practise this exercise, counting in your head evenly and slowly, to help you with the rhythmic patterns at letter 'B' of this piece.

(b) BREATH CONTROL

This piece needs lots of air and support, and good breath control. Try this exercise as slowly as you can, keeping the note going right to the end of the second bar.

(c) VIBRATO

This piece requires a good vibrato. There are a few ways of producing vibrato: try moving your jaw slightly up and down, or gently shake the trumpet back and forward. In this exercise, increase the vibrato as the note gets louder and decrease for the decrescendo.

6. Puerta del Sol

TONGUING WORKOUT

Fast tonguing is easier if the tip of your tongue starts on the roof of your mouth, away from your teeth: think 'd' rather than 't'. If you feel adventurous, try double tonguing—think '*da-ga*' for the semiquavers (♫). With your metronome set to ♩ = 110, continue the pattern in *Ex. i* by working up the E♭ major scale to a starting note of A♭; then immediately come back down the scale, as shown in *Ex. ii*. Play these examples boldly and decisively.

Ex. i

single: d d d d d
double: d da-ga d d   *etc.*

Ex. ii

7. East Broadway and Jefferson

ORNAMENTS

Inflections and ornaments are used a lot in klezmer performance and can be added in many different situations. For instance:

is an embellishment of:

In the piece the grace notes are written as semiquavers (♫), but they are sometimes played even faster, as in *Ex. i*. Try playing it, starting slowly and gradually building up speed.

Ex. i

Here is another type of ornament, which sounds like laughing. You'll find it at letter 'B' of this piece. To play this ornament, swallow, or choke, the sound of the fall on each note. Practise with *Ex. ii*.

Ex. ii

E. Europe
Cuba

8. Jugando con el son

THE CLAVE PATTERN

This tune has an underlying rhythmic skeleton called a 'clave', shown in *Ex. i*. Practise clapping it along with CD track 16.

Ex. i

Notice in *Ex. ii* how the rhythms in the tune match up to the clave. Often the beginning of the second bar is anticipated (shown with *), and there is emphasis on beat 'two and' or on the last beat of the bar. Sing the phrases in *Ex. ii* while clapping the clave pattern. Start slowly, gradually building up speed until you reach ♩ = 152.

Ex. ii   (section A)

9. Rainy Season

GAUD MALHAR RAGA

This piece uses the Gaud Malhar raga, based on F. Typical movements between pitches include 4 sliding down to 2; flat 7 sliding to 5; and the pattern 4, 5, 6, natural 7, 8. *Ex.i* shows the shape of the raga.

Ex. i

Ex. ii shows characteristic phrases from the raga. Try playing it to get the feel of how the raga sounds.

Ex.ii

In the last six bars of the piece you can see a '*tihai*', which means a phrase played three times. The second repetition has a different emphasis as it starts halfway through the bar. Here is another example of a *tihai* for you to try:

Ex.iii

10. Anikulapo, Kini Tuntun

AFROBEAT RHYTHMS

Clap these rhythms along with CD track 22 until you find them easy. *Ex. i* is the skeleton of a lot of African music, and *Ex. ii* builds on this rhythm. The rhythms at letter 'C' are also related to these rhythmic patterns. Next, try playing the groove in *Ex. iii* along with CD track 22.

Ex.i   *Ex.ii*

Ex.iii

31

11. August in Guča

(a) ORNAMENTS

Serbian brass players use ornaments all the time. They find all sorts of alternate
fingerings to make this easier and can create a short grace note with the flick of a finger.
In this style of music, the ornaments are played 'long-short, long-short'. The group of four
semiquavers (♫) that appears first at letter 'A' should be played as the ornament shown in
Ex. i below:

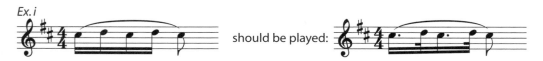

Practise playing these ornaments using *Ex. ii*:

(b) SCALES

Ex. i is the scale that forms the basis of this piece, while *Ex. ii* is the scale used at
letter 'D'. Try playing them:

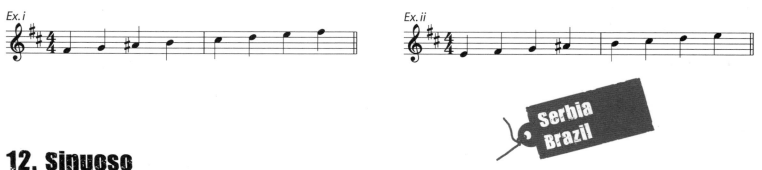

12. Sinuoso

(a) CHORINHO EXERCISES

This piece moves through a number of different keys. With your metronome set to ♩ = 68,
practise moving from one to another by playing this sequence of scales without a break:

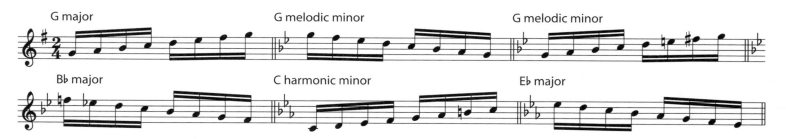

(b) SAMBA RHYTHMS

Practise the samba rhythms after letter 'C' with the arpeggios in the exercise below: